Eugen Nacht-Stroe

THE KING'S TRAP

Or how I understand theather

CoMedia

Collection: CoMedia
Cover: Stelian BIGAN
Cover illustration: Horaţiu MĂLĂELE

CIP description of the National Library of Romania
NACHT-STROE, EUGEN
   The King's Trap : or how I understand the theatre /
Eugen Nacht-Stroe. - Bucureşti : Integral, 2025; foreword by
Ileana Pernesh Danalache. - Bucharest: Integral, 2025
      ISBN 978-606-992-762-5

© INTEGRAL, 2025
Editor: Costel POSTOLACHE
DTP operator: Gelu ISPAS
Printed in România

Eugen Nacht-Stroe

THE KING'S TRAP

Or how I understand theather

INTEGRAL

Eugen Nacht-Stroe was born in Bucharest on April 21, 1952, son of Stroe and Rolanda. His father, N. Stroe, actor, author, composer and director, was one of the great stars of the Romanian revue theater and together with Vasile Vasilache he formed the "Stroe and Vasilache" couple. Rolanda Camin, his mother, was also an actress of the revue theater. From early childhood, Eugen lived and grew up in the world of the stage. He studied at the German High School in Bucharest and, after graduating, he took the entrance exam to the Theater Institute, I.A.T.C. He managed to get into Eugenia Popovici's class one year later.

In December 1977 he emigrated with his family to Israel. He learned Hebrew in record time. He did his military service in the Army Theater (*Teatron Zahal*) and then he was hired as an actor and assistant director at the National Youth Theater in Tel Aviv, directed by the famous actress Orna Porat. In 1986 he was invited to Paris, where he collaborated with the great director Peter Brook. On his return to Israel he founded an experimental theater group in Yaffa. In 1990 he founded the theater department at the Experimental Arts School in Givataiim. In this position he taught, directed, wrote and composed all the school's productions. In 2001 he founded his own theater school *The Eugene Nacht Acting Studio* in the town of Shoham, where he has written, composed and directed over 60 theater productions, participated in 10 theater festivals in Israel and over 25 international theater festivals in Europe. The studio celebrated its 23rd anniversary this year. In 2013 he staged at the *Toma Caragiu* Theater in Ploiești (Romania) the musical comedy *Firfirika,* based on a text by N. Stroe, which ran for 11 seasons. He has written two biographical books published in Romania: *Stroe-Vasilache-Applause and Hello, here's Stroe!*

He is married to Etty and has three children: Eytan, Lior, Ady

To my lovely wife and children,
Etty, Eytan, Lior and Ady

Preamble

THE LUCIDITY OF THE LONG RUNNING ARTIST

The King's Trap?

Surprising title and I declare from the first lines that I don't want to reveal to the reader the content of this unusual approach, that will ultimately bring him the satisfaction of being a part of the artistic art "immersed" in the very special crucible which is the soul of the graciously gifted one. *The actor.*

I have repeatedly asked myself the question related to the inner state of the artist who comes before the audience, for a few hours, to offer himself "body and soul" to a fascinating, troubling, disturbing dialogue like no comments or an addenda. Because you make your work like the sculptors of Greek antiquity (if you still like to quote Aristoteles) in detail, in the silence of the workshop.

You left for the Land of Promise, the land of your ancestors, leaving behind a cultural space deeply impregnated with memorable successes, to which your father, the famous artist, N. Stroe, also contributed.

Directors, actors, who established themselves as reference names in Europe in the '70s important names that you did not forget, Lucian Pintilie, Liviu Ciulei, Lucian Giurchescu, that you took into your spiritual baggage. For your part, you left behind the image of a rebel willing to be the disciple of other great creators.

Actor, producer, director, teacher of Theater Art and, last but not least, a sensitive man. Subject to the joys, the sorrows, the mistakes, the questions. A man who begins his confessions willing to show a little more than we thought we can learn about that incandescent matter from which the artist's inspiration springs. I confess that I did not expect to find my colleague from I. A. T.C. "I.L. Caragiale, acting department in the position of "ex-cathedra" professor and I read the text breathlessly, with hungry curiosity and a kind of permanent inner fear driven by the desire to tell him: "Eugene Nacht, I believe that, page after page, you challenge the reader to accept with no comments your skill fully crafted version, after more than half a century of tireless journeys on the meridians of art, and would who stopped for a moment in the living stream of events that change the face of the world. The theatrical movement was renewing after the terrible forced break imposed by the Second World War.

Peter Brook was your mentor and I won't add anything more than, adventurous spirit, ex band kid at the Constantin Tanase Revue Theatre, you only changed the geographical place, keeping untouched the joy of the game, of the message sent to the people, night after night. An effort doubled by the unacknowledged sadness of being an ephemeral passage on the theater stage. You prove to us with convincing arguments that it was and remains the way to stop, for a moment, the merciless flow of time. You are not afraid to remind the years when you took a start from the beginning, building with talent a space of only yours, that you reinforced with a message that crowned your existence: don't lose in vain unique experiences, exceptional moments. Shakespeare and his unique characters, the performance in its final form, refined and, above all we find you, wielding like a true artist, the third energy: the theatrical act.

ILEANA PERNESH-DANALACHE
Theatre and film critic

FOREWORD

Writing a book about theater. Why? What for? For whom? A lot of doubt turmoil and indecisions. Until I came across a saying of Aristoteles: "Those who know, do, those who understand, teach the others." In the thorny journey through the universe of theater, a journey that began more than 50 years ago, I had the opportunity to meet many creative people and personalities, passionate, bored, impostors, and among them some dominant and inspiring figures. Constantin Marinescu, Catalin Naum, Stefan Tapalaga, Florian Motzu Pittish, Lucian Giurchescu, and, especially, Peter Brook. Motzu Pittish is the one who opened the theatrical horizon to me and made me aware of this name, Peter Brook.

Constantin Marinescu was my first director when, in my first year at the Theater Institute, he hired me and Sorin Medeleni and together we opened the theatrical season at Student Club, at the "Students House of Culture" in Bucharest. Master Tapalaga was my assistant and the only real teacher I had at the beginning of the Institute. I personally met Lucian Giurchescu only in Tel Aviv, when I was an actor at the National Youth Theater in Israel. He chose me to act in the theater's new production, *"Androcles and the Lion"* There, I was also his assistant director. I learned a lot from him. He came with a very dynamic and modern conception, and the other actors in the group tried hard to adapt to his level so high.

And last, but not least, the "wizard" of the world theater, Peter Brook. He is the one who, so to speak, changed my whole life. His performances but especially our many meetings and discussions on theatrical work, the lucky connection he made me with the teachings of the great philosopher G. I. Gurdjieff, all these produced in me a real earthquake, after which the elements of life were reset in a specific order which allowed me to understand life and, implicitly, theatrical work in a much fairer way. The train stations in the course of life are not as important as what was collected on the road, decanted, processed by the soul and brought to the gate of knowledge. A route traveled in parallel on the unknown side of the soul.

When I attended my first *workshop* with Peter Brook in April 1986, at the "Bouffes du Nord" theater, we were introduced to and participated to a series of fantastic theatrical exercises and experiments. I thought I was dreaming. How to do theater like Peter Brook? Just as simple as that! You do all those exercises from the workshop and that's it... Many questions had not been asked. "Why? To what? From where and where to?" A bunch of years had to pass, full of attempts to know myself more deeply, to discover the hidden mechanisms of life, the unwritten laws of the Universe, trials pigmented by unforgettable encounters with Brook, so that at some point the fog lifts and some deeper understanding emerges. Now I could say, trying to keep within the limits of modesty, that many inner and outer processes became clear and full of meaning.

I did not think at that time, that this was only the beginning…

THE KING'S TRAP
Or how I understand theater

> *"The play's the thing*
> *where in I'll catch the conscience of the king". "*

In one of the monologues spoken by Hamlet, in the famous and sad play of the great Will, he says: "The show will be the trap in which I will capture the king's conscience." This phrase is, in my opinion, the essence of theater. Theater offers this unique possibility to touch and to influence the audience conscience.

Each of us, in our everyday life, tries spontaneously to defend ourselves from the surrounding world in order to feel safer and, therefore, more at peace with ourselves. For this purpose, we build day after day, moment after moment, a strong wall around us. With this wall, with this armor, we act in the outer life.

This armor became an integral part of us. We wear it without realizing that we go with it at work, shopping, or having fun...

In the audience, comfortably sitting in the armchair and looking towards the stage, sometimes curious, the armor is on us, the wall separates us from everything around. It's our way of receiving life around us. Here comes the power of theater to penetrate through this shell. This possibility exists and has always existed. But how? In what way? What must be done to allow the show to invade the territory of our privacy? We often enjoy a theater performance. Sometimes it amuses us, it cheers us up, it makes us sad, it makes us think. Other times it leaves us indifferent or even annoys us or bores us. These are the normal reactions we have in this encounter with the show. But deeper, nothing was touched. There, deep in our soul, everything remained intact. There, where a pure vibration still lives.

How do we build "the King's trap?"

How do we succeed in penetrating the twisting labyrinth of our deepest being?

HOW DO WE START, BEFORE WE START

Before taking an action, on the thorny road to professional achievement through learning and unlearning, it is necessary to stop a little in the space of awareness and self- knowledge. These are not "big words in the wind". The awareness is an inner process very difficult to achieve and, at the same time, very possible. Awareness is a kind of awakening to reality, from a somewhat hypnotic sleep, in which we dream that we are conscious and that everything is alright, an inner mechanism that protects me from the surrounding aggression and that gives me the feeling that I'm fine, that everything is fine, that you can stay calm. A pleasant illusion. It is necessary to wake up to reality.

The act of awareness can help us a lot. This practice must be done voluntarily and over time. Why awareness is so important in the actor's work? This act of awakening is not important only by itself. This act also brings with it an inner opening to another energy, of a much finer and different quality that can enter the body. It can touch the viewer's heart. And a lot can happen there. I don't have to get carried away by the energy of the "acting". I must be aware every moment of what is happening to me.

Take for example the following exercise. With a group of actors walking in the scenic space. At first my attention is drawn to the other actors around me. Looks, smiles, jokes... Little by little I try to isolate myself from those around me and start to focus on myself. "I focus on myself" - it's too "broad". I have to do some precise actions. Otherwise I get lost in my thoughts. For example, while walking through space, I try to be aware of the air I breathe, in and out through my nose. All my attention is focused to the act of inhaling and exhaling. Then I can move on. I can try to feel the difference in sensation between the air I breathe in and the air I breathe out. All these, just that I walk around the room.

Another effective exercise in the effort to become conscious on the stage is the following one. We play a scene from a play or, simply, do an improvisation. In two, in three, as we want. From beginning to end we say out loud all the actions we do (including entrances and exits). As much as it can amuse and disturb you, it makes you more attentive and aware of everything you do on stage. What can help me outside of the attention augmentation exercises, is to recognize that I am naturally in a "hypnotic" state and I sincerely want to wake up.

How to wake up again from a hypnotic sleep? What is actually, a hypnotic sleep? It is a state of the brain in which I see and know what's happening to me, I think I'm awake, but, in reality, I am carried away by thoughts, images and sounds, without realizing it. In other words, I'm actively walking, staying, talking but my mind is totally elsewhere. This process is so natural, that I am super-used to this hypnotic state of mind.

To wake up, there are two possibilities: one, to get hurt. For instance, walking down the street in this hypnotic state, I will hit a pole. It will hurt, I will get a shock, and this shock will wake me up for a few moments. After that, little by little, I will return to the hypnotic state, until the future shock. Of course, you don't have to look for poles in the streets to get the shock.

The second way to wake me up is to organize some wake-up elements, like some kind of alarm clocks. A series of signals to remind me that I "sleep". As simple as possible.

The question is: how do I know I'm awake and not asleep? The most practical answer is: to have a body sensation. A sensation of the hand, toes, soles etc. Let's get back to the alarm clock. For instance, I put a colored label on my fridge. Every time I see it and want to open the fridge, I try to feel my hands. After I get a feel for them, I check which of the two I feel stronger, when does the sensation disappear. Or I set the cell phone to ring at a certain time. When it rings, I try to see where my thoughts were at that moment. Then I try to get a general feeling of the body.

OBSTACLES

Every theater man wants the performance to touch the heart of the audience and, if possible, as much as it can. But that, except for a few shows, doesn't really happen. If we would refer to the idea of "The King's Trap", the question comes naturally: Does the show I saw manage to touch me deeply? Did it manage to stay deep in my soul, to produce some change? No? Why? The text is not good? The actors do not play well? The direction is not successful? The sets or costumes are not well made? The audience is stupid? The seats in the hall are not comfortable? In the hall it is too cold or too hot? Why? Is this legitimate desire an absurd one?...

Let's look together for the obstacles that stand in the way of the accomplishment of this desire. Let's start with the spectator. He is the most innocent. He comes to the theater and wants to have fun, to experience emotions, to be transported to a world different from his own... He sits in the hall and waits for the miracle. That's his role in this equation. In this early moment, when the curtain has not yet risen, the one who waits in his seat is still far from the miracle of the show: the contact between the two energies, that of the show and that of the audience. The spectator came to the theater from the midst of the everyday life in which he lives. His brain is still hardwired to everything that stirred him, amused and excited him during the whole day. Three quarters of it is there, in the events he experienced during the day. And, if what he will see on the stage will not affect him to any extent, he will remain there all the time. In this case, everything depends on what will happen on the stage.

What happens on the stage?

The stage – the physical space where the show takes place. With curtain, without curtain. The curtain that hides behind it the secrets of the show, creates a moment of mystery and, with it, an impulse of curiosity on the part of the audience. But, at the same time, it also becomes a means of separation between the performance and the spectator.

The spectators are in the hall. On the other side of the curtain are the actors. Two different entities, that must not meet. By removing the curtain from this combination, the audience will see at first what should have been hidden behind it. This creates some proximity between the stage and the hall. But another problem comes into play here. The law of the stage says that those on the stage decide the direction in which the spectator will think and direct his imagination. Which means that what he will see on the stage when he enters the hall will immediately act upon him. So, in a way, his imagination will be directed to the show that will start soon. Everyone is happy. The spectator receives a direction of thought, the actors enjoy the security they long for when meeting the audience, and the show begins.

But, there is a big *but*, a true encounter does not occur with preconceived ideas. In that magic moment when the energy of the spectator meets the energy of the actors, the meeting space must be as clean as possible. The contact occurs for a moment. This moment is decisive. I don't know anything you don't know anything and we both risk something. If we both know what awaits us, the real meeting does not take place. It will be of course, a meeting, but only one of complacency. The risk coefficient is high. The risk of being in front of the unknown without weapons of defense.

It's precisely at this moment where the real possibility lies. To this meeting, we, who invite the guests, must definitely prepare like a lover who invites his girlfriend to his house and tries to make everything perfect. How do we do our best? We do a performance that is perfected in the smallest details, a performance that we have repeated dozens of hundreds of times, we remember every detail and reproduce it exactly in front of the audience. So to speak, we come super-prepared for the meeting. But maybe, this super preparation, this perfect gift, will *not* allow the viewer to enter the whirlwind of the show?

This does not mean that we have to offer the public an unfinished show. The possibility must be searched much more deeply. For what we prepare, how do we prepare? We are getting ready to show the public our "great show or to actually meet him? We are getting ready to prove to the audience how talented we are and what an amazing show we are offering them? Or maybe we prepared to share with the spectators in the hall an experience lived during rehearsals, an attempt that we will redo in their presence? Everything is based on a play of energies. The show is just a form that this energy takes. There are many levels and qualities of energy. This is a very important truth. In order to penetrate the armor that the spectator wears in everyday life, a different level of energy is needed. The whole process of creating the performance must be rethought. From the first reading of the text to the last rehearsal. Peter Brook was talking about the "empty space of the stage. But how do we create an empty space in mind and heart in order to start something new, truly new?

THE ACTOR'S WORK

A professional actor must first be able to navigate the ocean of energies between scenic and public space. There are basic things they need to learn and practice in drama school. The sistem of hiring non- professionals, because they are more "authentic", as in the cinematography of the 60, has no place in the field of theater, where the show is produced only once in front of the public, and this experience is repeated many more times. Actors must be trained. By a teacher, by a school, by a group. Experience tells us that by himself, he will not reach the target. Only having a solid foundation, the actor can begin his journey to the unknown shores of the soul and the surrounding world. Because the real journey is beginning just now. How do we adress to these two worlds: the inner and the outer? With what kind of attitude? In 1986, at the *"Bouffes du Nord"* theater, in Paris, Peter Brook, in full season with the *Mahabharata* show, organized a *workshop* presenting his personal work system with actors. One of the journalists in the audience asked the great director which is the secret of the immense success of his theatre group, which at that time was considered as one of the best in the world. One of the actors, Maurice Benichou, stood up and said a single phrase:

"This is because we are very modest people". This apparently unimportant phrase hides in it a great secret of life: it is the modesty of man that allows him to open himself to the secrets of life. In the theater in the actor's work, this quality exists quite rarely. And its lack causes many train derailments. "I am the most"... "Look at me and be amazed", "your generation has never seen such a great actor"... "such a great actress"... This kind of actors does not have the possibility to become, to advance on the road to scenic truth. Their ego stops them from correctly deciphering reality. And something else. The desire of the actor to "show" himself in front of the public is one thing, and modesty is another. I have a conclusive example in my family. My father was a famous actor and director in the revue theater in Romania. He enjoyed a great celebrity. But he was a very modest man. The stage was for him the place where he could delight and excite the audience. The inner modesty, the true modesty, not "the performed" one, allows the actor to realize this cruel truth, that every step forward opens my horizon a little more and makes me understand how small I am in front of this immensity called "life". With this understanding, comes the desire to know more, to improve myself, to reach something that I cannot define, but, that I feel is somewhere and maybe it's waiting for me. Modesty and respect for colleagues and public are the weapons with which I can win. Let's not get confused. The stage qualities are indispensable to the actor. They are the starting point. An actor who thinks he knows everything, that no one can teach him anything is, in my opinion, a lost actor, even he is known and maybe, famous. This belief that I and only I know what must be done is a wall that rises in front of the actor and stops him from seeing what is hidden in the big world. What I have personally learned in this field is that for any step you take, you must prepare, to prepare something. A quiet moment of silence, of concentration, a decision, and then I take the step. But here comes another element that always makes me derail in another direction. This element controls my life from the shadows: FEAR. Fear that I do not see, that I am not aware of, but that is deep in my heart. This fear usually leads me to the land of comfort and self-assurance. Where I have been before, I know the landscape and feel safe. I will repeat and, in a way, I will try to reconstruct a moment that existed in the past, a memory.

I am deluded by illusions. Every moment in everyday life happens as a result of something that happened before. It is a *result* of something that took place within my being. And now, because of my hidden fear, I try to "relive" the result. It doesn't work. Even Stanislavsky advised the actor not to play the *result*. The moment I become aware of this truth, a new possibility is born. Fear is there all the time. Hidden deep in my soul. Sometimes I feel it, sometimes I don't. Like a pain in a part of my body that I have carried with me for years and which has become a part of me and as such, accustomed to it, I no longer feel it. We cannot fight this element of fear. It is too deeply ingrained in me.

What to do? I can build another line in parallel of trying, of courage. When this parallel line becomes stronger than the fear line, I can take the true step forward. This is true for any inner human process.

The great philosopher G.I. Gurdjieff explains that man receives three kinds of food: food, air and impressions. All three are very important and without them man cannot survive. Of these three, the actor needs impressions the most. The baggage of impressions acquired during his lifetime will help him greatly in several ways. It will enable him to understand more about man and his relationship with the world around him, but above all it will help him to use his imagination, which is so important in this profession. Recognizing impressions as an important factor in the actor's work, it is necessary to emphasize that not everyone is affected by the impressions he receives from life. Or at least, not by all the impressions he receives. It all depends on how sensitive the receiver is. The actor must necessarily make a great effort to become very sensitive to the fine vibrations of his inner and outer world. He must self-educate himself so that something inside him vibrates when he receives impressions. The received impressions become memories in images, sounds, tastes and sensations. It is very simple to extract a photogram from memories and imitate it on stage. But that does not mean that you have been "inspired". "Imitation is not inspiration. Inspiration comes from imagination and life impressions are its food. Like playing billiards: you hit the cue ball which in turn hits the red ball, the important ball. Impressions, memories are the black and white balls. Inspiration is the red ball. Even the text of the performance cannot act on the audience directly. "Life is hard", "War is destructive for both sides", "Love conquers".... These phrases spoken on stage are worthless. You're red balling the audience. But indirectly, when the story, the atmosphere and the play act on the spectators, if they are launched, directed and weighed in the right way, then the idea I wanted to convey can appear in the mind and heart of the spectator. Performances that launch ideas, concepts and conceptions of life from the stage to the audience do not reach their destination. The audience has to understand from the context what is important. And this concept also applies to everyday life. All these elements do not come by themselves or on command. They have to be practiced over and over again. Each trial in this struggle brings you closer to the outcome. Fighting what? With unseen spirits? The people around you? Against fate that is against you?

Do not seek the enemy outside yourself. He lurks within your being. There are actually two enemies and they have names: habit and laziness. They stop you on the road to self-perfection. Habit inspires self-confidence. By doing the same inner gestures all the time, these gestures become more and more perfect and my ego is very satisfied. And that reassures me. The truth is I'm slowly becoming a very good robot. An automaton. Try a little exercise: brush your teeth with the other hand. It's very uncomfortable at first. With practice, it gets easier and easier. Getting used to it is safety first. And in facing the unknown, confidence is a comfort.

Even if it doesn't seem like it, laziness is also an energy. An energy that pulls you down. Pleasurable, soothing and creating inactivity. You can stay there. The train of life will take you in some direction, maybe not the direction you'd like, but somewhere you'll end up. Nothing stands still. Everything depends on your inner decision.

So, what do we do? How? To do something real, it's necessary that the inner world sees these obstacles and understands that they are obstacles to my development. Only then can something be "done".

The actor's "battlefield" is his body. It is everything he possesses. It is also what is presented to the audience. It must be worked. Physically, emotionally and intellectually. He will have to become sensitive, flexible and feather-light. In this body, energies of all kinds clash. You can't control them. They emit vibrations and we from time to time react to the result these vibrations produce on our body and being. That's all. The actor has an opportunity to step forward. He can learn to feel and listen to this body. It is a natural act. It is not "make-believe" as it was once said in the theater world. This interior act of being a conscious witness to your own life releases an energy of a much finer quality than the energy we transmit in everyday life. Of course, in order to realize this inner act, it is necessary to get rid of a number of obstacles that naturally oppose our desire. The "mechanical" obstacles: the endless chatter in our heads which, like a funnel, prevents us from realizing, from becoming aware of what we are doing. This chatter often directs our attention elsewhere. Then there is the habit of our body. Our bodies have gotten used to functioning physiologically, motorically, mentally and emotionally in a certain way. At any attempt by me to do something different, this body will resist. I will find myself in conflict. Am I able to stay on this "Battlefield"? It all depends on how much I want to take this step.

Another very important element in the actor's work is working with feelings. It is very easy to mimic feelings. For some spectators this pantomime of feelings is enough. But to "capture the conscience of the king" requires more effort. It requires an inner freedom to move from one state to another naturally. A freedom that allows you to "juggle" your feelings.

It's interesting to note how in a comedy the actor manages to exaggerate feelings with ease, whereas in a dramatic performance, expressing them becomes more difficult. This is because in a comedy the energy of acting and the joy of acting realize this inner freedom.

The inner tension blocks. This inner release of the actor is like a man putting on a pile of clothes. He will find it very difficult to move in space. He will have to peel off layer after layer until he feels more free: the muscular tensions of the body, the countless thoughts that are pounding in his head, the worries of everyday life, and so much more. Only then will he be able to enter the realm of feeling.

Today's actor must try to use his intuition as much as possible. And to use it, he must first develop it. What is intuition? Where does it come from? Is it something real or just a figment of our imagination? Is a woman more intuitive than a man? Is an artist more intuitive than a regular man? Such a small word and so many questions...

Intuition, an energy center inside our body, probably in the region of the solar plexus, transmits signals translated by our brain as "sensations". It seems that what intuition conveys is the objective truth of a situation. Einstein said that "The only thing of real value is intuition".

So, intuition... How do we develop it and try to use it in the actor's work? There are actors who have a highly developed stage intuition, which sometimes covers their intellectual gaps. But most actors need a lot of work with themselves to get to the level where this inner signal, intuition, tells them what is right and what is wrong. But there's a stumbling block. Inside ourselves. Our head. The thinking center in the region of the brain works non-stop 24 hours a day. And more than that. We've gotten used to the head giving us split-second answers. The body's machinery works perfectly and allows us to function like a robot, which for many of us is a relief. Because of this impediment, it is necessary to turn off the "automatic responder" from time to time to allow other energy to emerge. Through various exercises, with time, this is possible.

For example, a very simple but very effective exercise. A in front of B. A makes a movement towards B which is as abstract as possible, accompanied by a sound. B has to respond to A with another movement with a sound that is not pre-arranged. After a minute the roles change. Then each of the two does all the moves spontaneously. Simple, but.... What happens when I have to respond with another gesture with sound? As I said, the brain works without pause. Moreover, the brain works very fast. We have to understand that this brain, or part of it, is like a perfectly functioning machine. It is something mechanical that normally and spontaneously does this: it looks for answers to any question that arises. That's how we were brought up: "Put your mind to work!" And the mind solves everything. But not in our case. Back to the exercise above. I must respond immediately to the sound and movement that has been made in front of me. If I wait for more than half a second, my brain will produce the image and sound it invented. If I react immediately, I react before my brain does. In this case, the brain will not make an effort and will not consume energy. Therefore, during the exercise, by saving the brain energy, the remaining, unconsumed energy will produce a pleasant state of well-being.

Later on, we can strive to be more attentive and more sensitive to these signals we receive from within ourselves. One proposal would be to try to see what we "feel" and not what we "think" about one thing or another, because usually our head will immediately give us its answer.

I will give an example from Carlos Castaneda's book *"The Teachings of Don Juan"*. It's an exercise I often do with my students. Walk around the stage and sit on the floor. Try to feel if this place you are sitting on is the most appropriate place in the stage space, if it is the 'ideal' place to sit. Stand up and look for another seat. Again, try to feel if you have found the most appropriate place in the space. After a few tries, you will decide which is the best place. Or another exercise is an exercise where you don't use your brain but your intuition. Two actors face each other. One makes an abstract body movement. The one in front responds with a sound. Or vice versa. Since there is no logical connection between the body movement and a sound appropriate to that movement, the brain can't help me. I have to look for the answer somewhere else inside me.

Exercises to stop the flow of thought require quickness and alertness. Exercises to develop intuition, on the other hand, take time.

A final important aspect of the actor's work is when he "jumps from one horse to another". How? Throughout rehearsals, the actor stores a lot of information, sensations and feelings in his mind and heart. Then comes the set. Then come the costumes. Then the lights, the background music and finally the audience. During all this a subtle process is going on in his subconscious. And if there is a strong desire and enough inner freedom, then the leap from one horse to the other takes place. In other words, the actor goes from his personality, which holds him prison-like, to the personality of the character, while having the inner freedom to return to his own. It is a magical, inexplicable moment. This leap gives the actor a particular freedom and pleasure. This is the key moment that the greatest playwright and theorist of the Japanese Noh Theater, Zeami, defined as "the opening, the blossoming of a flower". There is no technique or method to reach *this* moment. What can we do is simply prepare the ground for *this* leap.

THE PRESENT MOMENT

It often happens that a director or a teacher gives you a seeming innocent indication, that, through its innocence, flies past you without Knocking you down, or, at least, without touching you. The indication itself may be very valuable. But putting it into practice is nearly impossible, in the physical and mental state in which you are, at the moment of listening. Back in the 1960s the more unskilled theater directors used a saying that, in their theatrical understanding, solved everything: "Put in more feeling! ". I am not referring to such indications. An indication such as "play the present!" may be very true, but impossible to achieve without prior preparation. What do you mean "prior"? What's so complicated? Etc, etc...

The essential problem is that, in our everyday life, we live in the past, with the memories of past life experiences, and in the future, through our dreams and imagination of what we think will be. It is an automatic behavior, a habit of ours, that we carry with us from early childhood. This is how we have formed and this is how we continue.

And now let's go on stage. The stage, the audience, the performance, and the actor's sincere desire to act well, to be appreciated makes the actor turn to the "toolbox" he is used to working with, to the "tricks" he has used in the past and which have produced positive results, to the stage "tricks" he has learned throughout his career. And this will bring the long-awaited success. Very nice. Yes. But this acting, in this situation, is an acting "in the past". Using all these elements to succeed, we are automatically teleported to the past. We are on stage, the audience is in front of us, we are playing, but our being, without realizing it, is in the past. We want to live the moment, we want to vibrate, to feel, every time we want this. We think of the stage directions, of the way we learned to act, of everything connected with the past. My head, my body is trapped in the past. And this moment on stage, this unique moment, is lost. It goes unnoticed, both by me and by the audience. I read somewhere the following phrase: "Our life is like a boat floating down a river in one direction, but the oarsman is always looking in the opposite direction". Very true for both everyday life and theater.

Living the present moment is a state of mind. A unique moment, that does not come by chance. A unique moment, that must be prepared. A target, a goal to be reached. Through various exercises there is this possibility of disconnecting from the past moment with all its memories and grasping the present moment. A very simple possibility is to try to feel my body, or part of it, to feel my breathing, to try to be aware of everything that is happening to me in this moment. This effort will bring me back to the present moment. Practiced many times, I will easily be able to realize this shift from dreaming about the past or the future to the present moment. In this moment, another quality of attention arises. I realize what is happening to me in that moment, what is happening to those around me. This moment appearing on the stage transmits to the audience, as I said before, an energy of a special quality.

All this effort to come to the realization of the present moment, is an effort of cleansing, of throwing away negative feelings, especially fear, memories, playing techniques, personal successes and failures, illusions in which we believe so much... And only after that, there is a chance to reach a stage, where we can live "the present moment". Theoretically it's not hard at all. But, as they once said, practice kills. Nobody wants to get rid of all that "baggage" they believe in so much, which gives them security and peace of mind. A bird in the hand is worth two in the bush. It takes a lot of courage in this battle with myself. It takes a lot of honesty with myself, and of course, modesty.

All this effort is possible. It is a practical effort that requires patience and time. But it is worth it.

A SMALL PARANTHESIS: TO KNOW AND TO UNDERSTAND

"Knowing" and "understanding " are two different things. Not everything I know, I understand. "To Know" is to store informations in memory. Understanding is an internal process, in which something inside me suddenly reveals a secret. Understanding is a very fine and fresh energy. I met a lot of young people who studied theater and acquired a lot of knowledge in the field. But they didn't understand this "knowledge" because what was missing from this inner process is the life experience, the rich gallery of personal lived experiences. All these experiences bring with them yet another drop of understanding, another small piece in the great puzzle of understanding life. What was missing there was the baggage of successes and failures, of happiness and despair and the constant quest to find the spark of life. But that young man is 100% sure that he knows and understands everything. Why? What makes him believe this lie? What is expressed at that moment is his ego. Our ego is a cloud of illusions. It's a kind of dream I live in permanently. My ego works as a buffer between me and the world around me. It's a wall I built to feel protected from those around me.

A strong wall. On one side of the wall is the surrounding world, and on the other side is me. "Me"? Who is "I"? If I take off my mask, all my illusions and ideas, what's left? Is there something there? Maybe.

Actually, yes, there is something there. But something small: the tiny spark that brought me to this world. It is so small, that you hardly notice it. When I want to look at myself, this spark is invisible next to the huge creature called "Ego". When we are children, our "Ego" is small. As we get older, he gets bigger and stronger, until he slowly, but surely, becomes a monster. The monster demands more and more attention and energy from me. What to do? How to eliminate the monster? Do I really want to eliminate it? Of course not. Because I have become the same monster. It makes me feel good, important, loved, appreciated, wanted, unique. My "I" completely identifies with the monster called "Ego." If I destroy it, if I destroy this wall, everyone will devour me. Therefore, the little spark beyond the wall barely flickers and longs for a touch of attention. It all depends on how much I understand this inner phenomenon, and, if so, how much I want to be really "real". If I find in myself a sign of skepticism towards the "dream" I live in, if I feel deep down a small and painful sign of longing for a forgotten paradise, then maybe there is a chance to wake up. My monster, my "Ego", is so important, that I give it all importance. A great sage from long ago said:

"Within us is a wolf and a lamb. Which will survive? The one we feed more."

When I buy a new car, I give it my full attention, I fall in love with it It becomes the focus of my life. Objectively, it is a bunch of tin, paint, glass and all kinds of devices, whose role is to take me from one place to another. That's all. Everything else happens because I treat it with too much enthusiasm and identify with it. I slowly become the machine. If I stop giving so much importance to my ego, if I stop believing so much in the lies I tell myself, the monster will become a mouse. And then what's left? I forgot about the little spark behind the strong wall. It is called *my essence*.

THE ROLE OF THE SHOW IS TO SUGGEST

One of the big differences between theater and cinema is that the film presents you everything exactly as in reality. Even *science fiction* films or cinematic fantasies present their reality, in every little detail. In this case, the viewer does not set his imagination in motion. He receives everything on a plate.

In theater it's different. They came to the conclusion that, in theater, the audience loves to set their imagination in motion. It is his hidden desire. It's his way of participating to the show. By the '60s the tumultuous years of the social and artistic movements, there was a fashion in the theater to allow the audience to take part in the performance on stage. The desire to make the spectator the protagonist. A famous example is the musical *Hair*, where the audience was invited on stage to dance with the actors. Peter Brook is the one who understood this desire for public participation. The audience participates in the theatrical event by activating their own imagination. If the performance on the stage gives the spectator in the hall a suitable hint, he will, spontaneously, set in motion his imagination, the act which will complete in his mind the whole stage picture. Sometimes I do the next experiment in front of an audience: I draw a tree on a sheet of paper. Then I show the drawing to the audience. Everyone answers: a tree. No one says "a piece of paper on which you drew a tree". The imagination was set in motion. It immediately saw the tree. Interesting. In theater, it is necessary that the performance on the stage, its form, allows the spectator's imagination to undertake this inner act. It is necessary for the performance on stage to leave the spectator a minimum of freedom of inner movement. Everything I wrote here refers to the images transmitted from the stage to the viewer. The text of the performance as well as the entire scenic creation, can also contribute to this suggestive action. It is very important to consider the spectator as an active element of the performance and, at the same time, it is important that the performance on stage does not issue precise directions and conclusions. The role of the show's creators is to construct this labyrinth of images, ideas, feelings. Let the spectator enter and then exit this labyrinth. What he will think, feel and understand is his problem.

Another issue is the viewer's inner openness to the performance. In other words, in what manner does the spectator receive the show, how free is he from prejudices, free from emotional contractions, thoughts, memories and images, to absorb as much as possible from the show presented in front of him. At this point, the creators of the show can prepare the ground to bring the audience to some inner opening. I remember a funny incident from my student years, that can serve as an example of extreme openness to the show. I was in a camp of the Art Institutes, in Suceava (a city in northern Romania). We were taken to a nearby village to witness a folk dance festival at the cultural center. On the way, in the bus, there were many jokes about the "show " we were going to watch. We arrived at the venue, laughing "under our breath" at what we were going to see. We were greeted by the organizers, not with bread and salt, but with bacon, onion and tzuika, the traditional plume schnaps in Romania. In a quarter of an hour, we all were in high skies, and the folklore show we watched, a real triumph. An extreme example, as I said before I don't think it's necessary to get the audience drunk before the show. Although, in some cases, it would help (if not the public, at least the critics). But we can replace the tzuika, onion and bacon with other elements more suitable for the theatrical mood.

SEVERAL LINES IN PARALLEL

The inner effort of the actor in the field of concentration, of memory, of the body energy and the energy of emotions does not influence and does not act in one direction. Unlike those who believe that what is not seen, does not exist, or that what I do not know , does not exist, I maintain that, in this effort of the actor, several lines develop in parallel The actor is not aware of certain inner processes that take place within his being, but he can see at some point the results of them. The actor's work, in the educational system, during rehearsals and during the performance, is an inner process that continues its line of development depending on the purpose, the tools you use and the level of understanding of what you are doing and experiencing. But it is a process. You start at point X and end up at point Y. You do the outer and inner actions you need to do. For example, when preparing the show, outside of working with the director, you try to use your memory, imagination, concentration, remembering lived experiences, to succeed in creating a believable and, perhaps, even a charming character. But what we don't realize is that the the energy vibrations of our efforts also act upon the energy centers, the brain center and the emotional center. We are not aware of these inner processes. They act and influence our existence. They operate all the time, even when we make no conscious effort. Parallel to the efforts we make, another invisible line, unseen, develops and leaves its mark on all the activities we undertake. All these processes can bring us to the moment when something authentic and right appears. Sometimes we feel that we are not making any progress in "our struggle. We are not aware that "the struggle continues". It is very important not to force the struggle. The processes in us do not develop at the pace we think and want.

APPEARANCES ARE SOMETIMES DECEIVING

I sometimes watch actors play in movies or in the theater. Sometimes their acting convinces me and I am slowly transported into the world of creation. But often this process does not take place. Good actors, bad actors, convincing, unconvincing... I tried to understand what is going on with this phenomenon. You look at their acting on the screen or on stage and you think: they act well, with energy, focused, they move smoothly, they deliver their lines to the second, without mistakes. Everything seems perfect and we can only enjoy the performance to the full. But still.... However, what helped me to better understand what was happening in this perfect love affair were the telenovelas on the DIVA channel. I was looking at the talented actors who were playing in these series and suddenly I had a revelation. Their acting is outwardly perfect but inwardly superficial. There are viewers who are satisfied with this precise acting with assurance. They are used to it. They are satisfied and sometimes even "touched". Looking at it from the point of view of the energetic vibrations that the actor produces in this case, they cannot penetrate deep inside the spectator. These superficial vibrations will resonate something similar inside the spectator. They will fail to penetrate the inner defense shell. Let's not forget that it is the quality of the vibrations, not the quantity. Every actor seeks to find, to discover the character he will play. Some use the same tricks they have used before and it turned out well. Others sincerely try to discover the images, the impulses, the thoughts that bring him closer to the character. Al Pacino made an entire movie about the search for the character Richard III. It is as if we drill with an imaginary probe into the interior of our soul. Usually, the drilling stops at a shallow depth. There, inside us, it's pretty dark and it's hard to spot the precious stones. Besides the darkness, we get tired. We forget about it. Holy convenience speaks for itself. Or, we simply cannot penetrate this hidden world. And then we say the game lacked depth. Many great actors achieve this from their special intuition which, somehow, reaches the great depths of the soul in other ways and brings them the answers with speed. But if this "drilling" work is done correctly, the vibrations will be of a different quality.

THE MASTER BUILDER MANOLE AND THE ACTORS

Master Manole is a legendary figure in Romanian folklore, known for his role as a skilled master builder. The story revolves around his efforts to construct a monastery on a difficult site. Each time he and his team built the walls, they would collapse, leading him to realize that he needed to make a sacrifice to ensure the building's stability. Ultimately, Manole decides to sacrifice his wife, Ana, burying her in the foundation of the monastery. Thus, the monastery stood firm, and Master Manole became a symbol of sacrifice and dedication.

Who participates in the actor's play? Mind, body muscles, his energy, his emotions. That's it. An old story with the wise Mulla Nasrudin or as he was known in Romania, Nastratin Hogea: Mulla Nasrudin knew how to prepare a colossal halva. His neighbor, after he tasted the delicious product, asked him for the recipe. Mulla kindly gave it to him. Two days later, the neighbor comes to him, very indignant because the halva was a mess. Mulla asks him: Did you use all the components I wrote you ? Absolutely all, everything in all the quantities you wrote me. And it didn't turn tasty, replies the neighbor. To which Mulla added: Did you put something of your being? No. Well, that's it! I'm not remotely Mulla Nasrudin. but I'd ask the actor: Did you put something of your being? A dubious question. What do you mean, "my being"? I put soul, enthusiasm, energy, knowledge. So I put. My being, my soul, is something very deep. You can't put it in. You can only sacrifice part of it to give it to the audience. Like Master Manole. Am I capable of such a sacrifice? Maybe it's too much. For what? A big question we must face. It is said that the act of creation requires sacrifice. Why? Can't it be done without sacrifice? What, are we in ancient times when people sacrificed to the gods? Of course not. But maybe something in my being has to be set aside to allow a higher energy to enter me.

The truth is, it's very hard to let go of something that I'm attached to. Almost impossible. But still possible. An essential question would be: How generous are you?

Without making room, nothing can get in. The great Grotowsky spoke of this sacrifice of the actor. Maybe it's true....

TO MAKE A DECISION

To make a decision in life is a very complicated inner process. At almost every moment we have to make a decision. If we let ourselves be carried away by inertia, we gradually fall into mediocrity. This mediocrity is a comfort zone for many. It requires no effort and gives you the pleasant illusion of safety. If you want to make a small or big decision, it is not enough to have the necessary courage. It is necessary to understand, to glimpse the inner processes that help or oppose a righteous choice. There is always this inner prism that reflects false information to my brain. Inside me my Ego acts, this ferocious beast that wants everything, thinks that everything is due to it and blinds me to the objective reality. My ego is my childhood companion, lives through me and I through it, unnoticed. Next to him, it does its work a kind of energy damper, a kind of armor which naturally protects me from the world around and which whispers to my soul: "Everything is fine. You are doing very well what you are doing. Take it easy". The third element is the most complicated and the most persuasive. It is the image I have on myself and which is hidden in the cellar of my soul. Most of the time it is false. It is the result of lived experiences, usually, in the beginnings of life and sometimes, during it. An image that part of me totally believes in. "I am just a child", "I am capable of nothing", "I am the center of the universe", "I am not owed anything", "I am given everything", "I am far below the level of others" and so on and so forth. All these elements form the prism through which the energy of attention makes its way to consciousness.

I remember how, many years ago, I really wanted to play in a show made by a very famous director, whom I admired a lot. I prepared assiduously for the *casting* I did the monologue I had prepared. I was not received But I was happy that I could do the monologue in front of that director. As if something deep inside me was whispering to me: "Who are you to be in the show? A foolish child..." There all my struggle ended. My self-image stopped me from going on.

If I understand all this inner process, all the obstacles to my decision, I can act otherwise. First, I need to see how this machine works. Then, quiet, alone with myself, to detach a little from everything that attracts me like a magnet, making me blindly believe in an untrue image. And, finally, to choose.

But often we don't have the necessary time to make a choice. Especially in our job. Sometimes just a few seconds. In such cases the only anchor in this ocean of energies are intuition and common sense. Many years ago, I went to Paris only to consult with Peter Brook about an important choice I had to make. Peter told me: "I can't give you any advice. If you want to know what *I* do in such cases, when I have to make an important choice, I let the question to "work upon me". After a while, an answer rises up to the surface. So true.

MOMENTS OCCUR INDIRECTLY

I said it in the previous pages. The result should not be played. Two and three make five. Five is the result. I don't come on stage and say "five"! The audience won't understand: you mean why "five"? Five is just the result. That's why we have to come on the stage and say: "Two and three". Let the audience answer in his mind: "Five". This example brings me to the thorny issue of experiencing feelings or states of mind. We can' play them directly. First because it's very hard to play "true feelings". "Fake" everyone knows. I remember a funny incident. I was with my college classmate the well known actor Eugen Cristea, in my sophomore year, at the home of our assistant in the acting class. We had to work on a text for the acting exam. The table was laden with schnapps and cakes. At one point, to help us get through our theater work, the venerable assistant let us in on a secret: "Hey guys, look at me. I lift my chin up and say, 'Mama was beautiful.' Watch my tears come to my eyes...." Of course we could barely contain our laughter. What *"precious" directions*.... OMG!

Then what do I do? How do I get to the real feelings? First and first, I don't try to play feelings. I mean I'm not trying to convince myself that I hate, that I love, that I'm scared, that

I'm destroyed. That attempt will only stress me out more. I have to understand that in my body, apart from bones, organs, muscles etc., activates a large amount of energy. I should rather imagine my body as a container filled with energy. There are many levels and qualities of energy. And, at the same time there are three main energy centers that oversee the activity of energy: the brain center, the emotional center and the moving center. In all this energetic mess negative thoughts, fear, anger, hate, jealousy and many more turn inner energy into negative energy. This negative energy blocks the flow of energy through the body and the flow of energy inward and out ward, I, as an actor, want to produce a real feeling on stage. This true feeling should arise from the emotional center. But my body, i.e. the container, is always blocked by negative energy. We don't see it, but we can feel the result in the muscles stuck, in the negative thoughts, in the feelings of dissatisfaction, of frustration. So, we must first relax the whole body, muscles, thoughts, sensations Then, so relaxed, only saying the text, can bring about the emergence of pure feeling. Indirectly. We do something to act something else.

SAVE ME, LORD, FROM TEMPTATIONS!

Almost all the time we hear this saying: The temptation, the devil's hand, devil stuck his tail... What is temptation? The woman, the drink, the card game, the drugs, the theft and more and more... The dramatic elements of life. The super-temptations. But the mini-temptations? Those temptations that we hardly even notice: a distracting thought, a sudden desire for something. a memory that comes back and doesn't go away... Small, almost imperceptible things, that seem so innocent.

When we start a journey, we create a goal, a target. It is very important to formulate a goal. Then we try to travel the path towards that goal, with the thought that we will soon reach what we set out to do. We make a plan. But we forget that, in that journey, life continues around us. Everyday life, with its hardships, with its joys, with its temptations. What I have learned from life, in these long years spent with it, is that our power of attention leaves us and returns at very short intervals. And when it disappears, another wave of energy enters our mind, that draws attention to it. This, on an intimate scale. On a larger scale, in the whirlwind of our struggle to achieve our intended goal, there are always temptations of all kinds that can distract us from the chosen path. And so we may find ourselves in a place, other than the one we intended. For example, I want to go shopping at the supermarket. I get dressed, I go out the door, I reach the street and there I see that it has started to rain. I go back home and take my umbrella. I'm thirsty. I'm going to drink a glass of water. The phone rings. A friend asks me for a phone number. I look for the number in a notebook on the deck and I give it to him. That reminds me I had to call a friend at work for a plumber's address. I call him, but he says he is busy how. He's watching the soccer match between Argentina and Uruguay. I turn on the TV and look for the soccer channel. I can't find it, but I come across a documentary film about the Inca civilization and it captivates me. After about an hour, my wife appears and looks at me and asks me: Why are you sitting, dressed like that in an overcoat, on the armchair?" And I'm like: "Right. Why did I get dressed?" That's how things work. What should I do? To live in isolation so as not to fall prey to temptations? Or to try to be aware of the fact that these temptations always appear and have the power to evade me from the path I set out on? And if I am aware of this phenomenon. I can try to be a little more awake and present to what is happening? The most important thing is not to forget the final goal. To remember it all the time, to put it in front of me, like a star in the sky that guides me.

I want to become a great actor. I work conscientiously. I am full of energy and self-confidence. A promising start. In time, the energy gets tired, thoughts of giving up appear, the fear of the unknown makes its presence felt, the old professional habits appear, the lack of patience make me choose the easiest path, and so, temptation after temptation, I arrive at another address. What's important is that, now and then, to stop. To take a step back and check to see how far I've traveled to reach my goal.

Not only the actor is in a position to fall victim to diffe-rent temptations. The spectator at the theater performance is in a similar situation. If the show does not interest him, if something is not clear, if something seems illogical to him, if the actor's acting is not convincing, our dear spectator will start thinking about something else: what he will eat at home, what he has to do the next day and so on. His attention will be transferred from the stage to his everyday problems. At this moment, I have lost this spectator until the moment when something new on stage will again draw his attention to it. Peter Brook often explained that the job of the director and actors is to stimulate the audience's curiousity every few mo-ments, so that these temptations do not divert their attention.

THE ACTOR LIKE AN ONION

Albert Einstein wrote somewhere that "education is what remains after one has forgotten everything he learned in school". Strange statement but, perhaps, true. To learn does not directly assume to understand. After school comes real life, and, in real life what can categorize me as an educated person is what I understood from everything I leared, together with the life experiences during school, that impressed me. In theater it can be even more acute. We learn, we accumulate sometimes, we understand what we have learned from this job. All these give me an inner security that I need so much in the tumultuous adventure that is Theater. Over time I accumulate more and more "weapons" with which I can fight to defeat the obstacles and enemies that stand in my way. Because, let's admit, after the first success, the envy and enmity of the others show their fangs. In this situation, in order not to fall spiritually, I'm more freaking out of the things I learned and accumulated. I hold them in my hand, like a toy that I don't want to part with. They are the weapons that help me succeed in this job. But on the thorny road to build the "king's trap", I find myself in armor and full of weapons, but far from that almost forgotten truth. The truth of life. A self-cleaning action is required. It's too much, and this too much prevents me from reaching the true vibrations of life. Like a hot air balloon that can't lift off the ground because it's too loaded. What must be done is a painstaking work of discarding, one by one, the weapons that served me. It is a very difficult moment. I believe in them, I am attached to them soulfully. I cannot give them up so easily. Attaching to ideas, to objects, to people and identifying with them is an almost automatic inner act and very harmful to my existence. In the Buddhist monasteries of Tibet, monks spend days at a time making beautifully colored sand mandala designs of rare beauty. When they are finally done, they destroy them. Fools? Not exactly. It's the inner work with attachment to objects, to their creation, it's the work with non-identification. These rituals help them, by practicing them constantly, in their struggle not to identify with what surrounds them and with themselves.

Returning to our sheep, as they say, when I unconsciously have to let go of something I feel attached such as my beliefs in acting, I get stuck. To let off these weapons is not only a cognitive problem. It is first and foremost a matter of the soul. The power, to give something up. Only then the actor will be able to shed the layers of habits and beliefs to which he is attached. Like an onion, you peel back layer by layer, until you get to the core. Its core coincides with the true vibrations of life within the actor.

THE MAGICIAN AND
THE RABBIT IN THE TOP HAT

A magician has to get the rabbit out of the top hat. He knows well that the rabbit is hidden in the top hat. He just has to pull it out to fool the audience. He'll say "Hocus Pocus Preparatus!" and the rabbit hops! He emerges into the spotlight to the enthusiastic applause of the audience. The actor is also like a magician He has to bring out of his 'top hat', i.e. the rabbit, i.e. the real game, the real feelings. But here comes a problem. The rabbit does not come out. If he also says "Hocus Pocus" what will come out will be a stage prop rabbit, a fake rabbit. I've always wondered where the actor gets his game from. I didn't learn something like that at the drama school. There, it was explained to me how the game starts from the head, with a thought, then goes through the belly to the heart and from there, it goes out to the public. I really liked this scheme at the time. Then, for days on end, I would analyse the play, the characters and split the stand of hair into four until I knew perfectly who he was and what he wanted. The next step was to play the role. But where do we get the rabbit from? I know the outline, the head is full of informations and thoughts about the play and the character and... what am I doing now? Where do I get the authentic play full of pure feeling? Which hat do I pull the rabbit out of? For the magician it is simple. He Knows exactly what actions to take to get the rabbit out. But me, the actor, what actions must I do? A very true and mostly practical question. I usually do what I feel, that is "what comes to me at that moment, and, if I'm lucky, it might turn out well. I have no idea what to do. No one taught me, I can resort to an external imitation of what I want to play, to which I can add the energy of excitement, and with that I've "left them gaping ". It could be like that. But that is not what we are talking about in this book. I retur to the essential question: where do get the rabbit from?

What I understood after many years is that *I can't get the rabbit out. The rabbit can get out on his own, without me taking it out.* Then the real question would be: What do I have to do to get the rabbit out? What do I have to do for the real acting to come out from my inside? A true result to this question cannot be reached directly, but indirectly. That is, I have to do something in order for something else to happen. Inside the actor there is a neuron, a fine and fresh energy that must create his play. I can't touch it directly or use it directly. I must "court it", warm it, give it water and warmth like a flower. I must understand this idea. I carry the character in my mind, I imagine him, I improvise, I go to bed with him, I let myself be penetrated by the words he says in the play, I put on his performance costume, I put on my hat. But most importantly, I don't force it. I don't resort to quick fixes. I let go, I release tension and panic, I give it a chance. What is interesting is that in parallel, something is working inside me, something I am not aware of. I have to realize that life is not only what

I see and understand. Most actions and phenomena happen without my noticing them. In this search for the character, somewhere inside me, something takes shape and may appear. And if it appears, the character was born on the stage, for the stage.

In his movie *"Looking for Richard"*, the great actor Al Pacino describes this process of searching for the character. But not to find him and use the things he finds. But to feed this energy hidden from my eyes.

The great master of theater, Peter Brook used to shorten the period of reading and analizing the text and instead organize with the actors a lot of improvisations on the text and the characters. These improvisations were supposed to help the actor "find" the character. For a long time I thought that "finding the character" meant finding in the improvisations gestures, energies, facial expressions that you could use in the performance you were going to play. In other words, to try to imitate in the performance, what spontaneously emerged during the improvisations. Again an imitation. Today I understand this process that happens in parallel, without my control, but that I can help. Perhaps an image could help. The image of a little man inside me who needs many impressions from outside to manifest himself. Through my hard work, little by little he will come to life and give me the soul of the character. I have no direct connection with this little man. I do my work and he is fed by the impressions coming from me.

THE INTERNAL ELEVATOR

Imagine an elevator inside the actor. With this elevator he descends into himself and from there he brings to the surface stills of his experiences, impregnated with feelings and states of mind. But every event in our lives is propelled into space by the vibrations of energy. It is these vibrations that influence the actor's imagination, and this process can give rise to the "real play". It all depends on how low the elevator can go. The depth of the descent depends on a number of factors: inner freedom, degree of self-satisfaction, tenacity, etc. In most cases, the elevator only goes down one floor. It is stopped by complacency, or stress or other psychological barriers. If we watch the actors closely, we can read on their faces the depth to which the elevator has descended. There is nothing more deceptive than a perfect performance by the actor: perfect energy, perfect voice, perfect diction, perfect feeling. Robot perfection. People generally love perfect things. But, as I said before, it all depends on the quality of the energy, not the quantity. This "perfection" will give off low-quality energy. Unsuitable to create the "king's trap". As in any field of acting, nothing comes without work. Nothing comes by itself. And in this process of work, it is not only the result that is important, but also the experience lived during this process.

TWO FOR TANGO

There are many one-actor theater shows. Monodramas, recitals, etc. And some are very successful. It takes a lot of courage, experience and talent to captivate an audience alone.

And then there are other shows with several actors, in which some of them act "alone". Every man for himself. In the old days, the show was initiated, organized and directed by a single actor. He would usually stand on stage in front and the other actors in the scene a meter or two behind. The "star" would deliver his lines facing the audience and the other actors would respond from behind. The audience was pleased because that was the custom in those days.

The relationship between two characters on stage is a very precious situation. A situation to which we must give our full attention. Especially if our goal is the king's trap. We can look at each other and enthusiastically say the text with different facial expressions. The audience will be satisfied. But as I said before, after the performance they will go home and forget, because the energy of the actors' acting failed to penetrate deeply. And that's quite normal. Each of the two partners was preoccupied with himself.

The meeting of two characters on stage is a moment with so many possibilities. Possibilities that many of the audience have forgotten in everyday life. That's why sometimes theater can remind us of what real life should be like. Working with a partner means creating together a shared energy, a shared universe. This energy will not appear on command. I have a long way to go in working with myself and with my partners before we can create this "common energy". It is necessary to take off from us, like a coat, a little of our egotism, of our desire to show off, of our arrogance. It is necessary to rebuilt in us the sense of curiosity. This sport of "living again the curiosity" is of great use in situations where you perform in a show dozens and hundreds of times, a situation in which the danger of automation is certain. Find in yourself that impulse of curiosity about those in front of you. Help each other. Be generous. But above all beware of clichés and artificial reactions. Do not be afraid. Look deeply into your partner's eyes. Try to discover what's hidden in them. Feel their breathing, their body vibrations. Trust him. And all without any connection to the character you're playing. This part of it is about breaking down the barriers between actors. Not all actors are friends with each other. If we don't make this effort to get closer, the relationship between the characters in the performance will be "fake". There are many helpful exercises to achieve this goal. For example, a simple exercise. The two partners lie on the floor, back to back. At first they just try to feel each other's back. What do they feel? Physical contact? Body heat? How does it feel to touch each other's back? Then, in stage two, each of the two in turn will make a sound, then a word. The one receiving the sound or word must make the same check as in the first stage. In the third stage the two partners will say the dialog, at first almost whispering, then louder and louder. Each of the two will perform the same check as in the first two stages.

Another possibility is a psychological exercise. I try to put myself in a state of curiosity. In this situation, I try from the beginning of the rehearsal period to find as many things in my scene partner that we have in common. Of course, both partners must do this.

Only then do we move on to the characters and what happens between them. In the end, if we have managed to share our unique experience with the audience, we have achieved our goal. In other words, we have discovered the path to theater creation. Just the way. The effort has to be repeated each time. With great labor, perseverance and patience.

INSTEAD OF "THE FINALE"

Everything I wrote in this book are not just some ideas about how I think the theater should be, but a series of conclusions following some theoretical researches, but, above all, practical. Reading this book and understanding it is a first step. It's like a door you've reached, but haven't opened yet. Will you open it?

Maybe what you've read is enough for you. Nothing pushes you from behind to open the door. What you read, what you understood, is enough. Everything will remain a memory that, like any memory, will disappear in time. It is not simple to put your hand on the handle and open the door. Because behind this door is a hard work, that requires a series of renunciations, that requires a special state of vigilance and, above all a lot of courage. It's a big risk. Is it worth? You will have to answer that for yourself. I can't convince you . Nor do I want to. I have only told you what is behind this door. But I think it's worth it. We are too intoxicated by a kind of theater so popular today, a theater of tumultuous energies of spectacular productions or exhibitionist actors. This drunkenness creates a state of pleasure. How to set aside pleasure... Here is an aspect that stopped me from writing this book for a long time: the fear that many people will not believe that there is another possibility, one that is much fairer, much truer. That possibility is there, all the time.

But, as the saying goes: "What's in your hand is not a lie".

What do we do?

Will we do it?

ADENDUM

INTUITION

Intuition is the human capacity to understand or know something without the need for evidence or logical, formal reasoning.

Intuition is based on sensations, perceptions and subconscious knowledge, and can be described as a *"gut feeling"* or a hunch. Intuition is often described as an immediate sensation or knowledge that occurs in a person's body, often without them being aware of the process, or the sources behind it.

Intuition can be developed and improved through increased self-awareness, self-reflection and practical experiences.

Over time, a person can learn to distinguish between their intuition and personal emotions or biases.

LOOKING INWARD

Looking inward can be a lonely journey, but at the same time, it can be one of the richest journeys we can take. Looking inward gives us the opportunity to get to know ourselves, to understand our emotions, thoughts and desires. At the same time, we can discover the things that drive our behavior and strive to become a more fulfilled and better person. Looking inward can also give us a clearer perspective on our relationships with other people.

However, the inward journey can sometimes be difficult and can take us out of our comfort zone. But once we get to know ourselves better, we can enjoy a more fulfilled and wiser life.

MIMETIC NEURON

The mirror neuron, also known as the *mimetic neuron*, is a special type of nerve cell that plays an important role in understanding and mimicking actions and emotions seen in other people. Mirror neurons are thought to be responsible for our ability to mimic other people's actions. When we observe someone performing a certain action, the mirror neurons in our brain become active, as if we were performing that action ourselves. This mirroring of actions helps us understand and learn from other people's examples.

Mirror neurons are also thought to play a role in empathy. When we see someone experiencing an emotion, mirror neurons can become active, allowing us to experience that emotion and understand what the other person is feeling. This is the scientific explanation for the phenomenon of the theater audience's identification with the performance being watched on stage in front of them.

THE HEART'S LITTLE BRAIN

The heart has been found to contain an independent and well-developed nervous system with more than 40,000 neurons and a complex and dense network of neurotransmitters, proteins and supporting cells.

Thanks to this elaborate circuitry, it appears that the heart can make decisions and act independently of the brain, and that it can learn, remember and even perceive.

The heart's electromagnetic field is the strongest of all organs in the body, 5,000 times stronger than that of the brain. It has been observed to vary with emotional state. When we feel fear, frustration or stress, it becomes chaotic. Then it returns to normal with positive emotions. The magnetic field of the heart extends two to four meters around the body, that is, everyone around us receives the energetic information contained in our heart.

The brain circuit of the heart is the first to process the information, which then passes through the brain to the head.

There are two types of heart rhythm variation: one is harmonious, with broad, regular waves and takes this form when the person has positive, uplifted and generous emotions and thoughts. The other is disorderly, with inconsistent waves. It occurs with the onset of negative emotions: fear, anger or distrust.

The brain waves are synchronized with these heartbeat variations, i.e. the heart, drives the head. The conclusion is that love is not an emotion, but an intelligent state of consciousness.

This new circuit does not go through old memories, its knowledge is immediate, instantaneous, and because of this it has an accurate perception of reality. It's like science fiction.

It shows that when people use their brains from the heart, they create a state of biological coherence. Everything is harmonized and functioning properly. It's a higher intelligence that is activated by positive emotions. Well, nobody seems to use it... It is a potential that is not being activated, but it is beginning to be accessible to many people.

This circuit can be activated by cultivating the qualities of the heart: openness to others, listening, patience, cooperation, acceptance of differences, courage. It is the practice of positive thoughts and emotions. It is essentially a matter of freeing oneself from the spirit of separateness and the three primary mechanisms: fear, desire and the instinct to dominate, mechanisms deeply ingrained in human beings, because they have served us in the past. How do we free ourselves from them? By taking a bystander position, observing our thoughts and emotions without judgment and choosing the emotions that can make us feel good. We need to learn to trust our intuition and recognize that the true origin of our emotional reactions lies not in what is happening outside, but inside us.

SOLAR PLEXUS OR ABDOMINAL BRAIN

The term "abdominal brain" is sometimes used informally to refer to the solar plexus. The solar plexus is a complex network of nerves located in the upper abdomen, behind the stomach. The solar plexus is considered the 'second brain' because of the large number of neurons and nerve networks present there. It plays an important role in the stress response and can influence emotions and mood.

What physiologists don't yet recognize, but ancient sages already knew, is that the solar plexus is the seat of the human emotional nature. In other words, that part that was popularly attributed to the heart in terms of emotions is actually the solar plexus, the center of our sympathetic system. The fact that there is a link between emotional states and the physical body is common knowledge.

We know that fear, dread, suspense are accompanied by a feeling of emptiness in the stomach. The heart beats faster when we are excited, angry or in love. In recent years it has been scientifically proven that emotional states have an impact on the body's organs, on its state of health, that the solar plexus is the seat of emotions, the place where they originate and are born.

Science thus indirectly proves what the Eastern spiritual masters have known for thousands of years: the solar plexus, the abdominal brain, the center of life, of vital energy, is the place where emotional sensations are born.

This means that if we want to regulate, control or direct emotions, we know where to start.

PHOTO

1. Feeling the body (Masca Theather Workshop 2012)
2. Speed of thinking (Masca Theather Workshop)
3. Relaxation exercise (Masca Theather Workshop)
4. Together with Peter Brook 2015
5. Divided attention (Shoam-Israel Theather Studio 2023)
6. Animating energy (Vratsa Bulgaria Festival 2011)
7. Attention exercise (Shoam-Israel Theather Studio)
8. Joint movement creation (Shoam-Israel Theather Studio)
9. Feeling the partner (Shoam-Israel Theather Studio)
10. Attention exercise (workshop Alba Iulia - Romania 2014)
11. Working with sticks (Shoam-Israel Theather Studio)
12. Divided attention (Shoam-Israel Theather Studio)
13. With director Lucian Giurchescu in Tel Aviv, 1984
14. Exercise of deep imagination (workshop Iassy, Romania, 2014)
15. Energy and relaxation (Vratsa Bulgaria Festival 2009)
16. Energy circle (Vratsa Bulgaria Festival 2009)
17. Attention exercise with sticks (workshop Iassy, Romania, 2014)
18. Keeping attention and body tension (Masca Theather)

16

17

Contents

Eugen Nacht-Stroe

CAPCANA REGELUI
Sau cum înțeleg eu teatrul

INTEGRAL

INTEGRAL PUBLISHERS
eintegral.ro   game of knowledge